The Basic Reading Comprehension Kit for
Hyperlexia and Autism™
Storybook

SO-EKL-086

by Pam Britton Reese and Nena C. Challenner

Skills	Ages	Grades
■ reading comprehension ■ vocabulary	■ 5 through 12	■ K through 7

Evidence-Based Practice

- Speech-language pathologists should enhance access to literacy and academic instruction for individuals with autism spectrum disorders (ASHA, 2006).

- For children with hyperlexia, use reading skills as a primary means of developing language. Teach reading comprehension specifically. Use written and visual models, as well as patterned language and fill-in-the-blank sentence forms (Kupperman, 1997).

- Text comprehension can be improved by instruction that helps readers use specific comprehension strategies, such as monitoring comprehension, using graphic and semantic organizers, answering questions, generating questions, recognizing story structure, and summarizing (NIFL, 2003).

- Students need to understand semantic connections among words (RCSLT, 2005).

The Basic Reading Comprehension Kit for Hyperlexia and Autism incorporates these principles and is also based on expert professional practice.

References

American Speech-Language-Hearing Association (ASHA). (2006). *Roles and responsibilities of speech-language pathologists in diagnosis, assessment, and treatment of autism spectrum disorders across the life span*. [Position Statement]. Retrieved March 16, 2009 from www.asha.org/policy.html

Kupperman, P. (November 1997). Precocious reading skills may signal hyperlexia. *Brown University Child & Adolescent Behavior Letter, 13*, 1-4.

National Institute for Literacy (NIFL). (2003). *Put reading first: The research building blocks for teaching children to read*. Retrieved March 16, 2009 from www.nifl.gov/nifl/publications.html

Royal College of Speech and Language Therapists (RCSLT). (2005). *Clinical guidelines for speech and language therapists*. Retrieved March 16, 2009 from www.rcslt.org/resources/RCSLT_Clinical_Guidelines.pdf

LinguiSystems®

LinguiSystems, Inc.
3100 4th Avenue
East Moline, IL 61244
800-776-4332

FAX: 800-577-4555
Email: service@linguisystems.com
Web: linguisystems.com

Printed in the U.S.A.

ISBN 10: 0-7606-0610-2
ISBN 13: 0-978-7606-0610-0

About the Authors

Pam Britton Reese, M.A., CCC-SLP, is currently working as a clinical supervisor at the Hearing, Speech, and Language Clinic at Ohio University in Athens, Ohio. She has worked with children with autism since 1997. Pam is also the author of *The Source for Alzheimer's and Dementia*.

Nena C. Challenner, M.Ed., is an assistant principal at Longbranch Elementary School in Midlothian, Texas. She has over 20 years of experience in general and special education.

Pam and Nena are also the co-authors of *Autism & PDD: Social Skills Lessons – Primary, Intermediate, and Adolescent*; *Autism & PDD: Concept Development*; *Autism & PDD: Expanding Social Options*; and *Autism & PDD: Safety*.

> "Beginning in the earliest grades, instruction should promote comprehension by actively building linguistic and conceptual knowledge in a rich variety of domains."
>
> (*Preventive Reading Difficulties in Young Children*, National Academy Press, 1998)

Edited by Lauri Whiskeyman
Illustrations by Margaret Warner
Page Layout by Christine Buysse
Cover Design by Mike Paustian

Table of Contents

Introduction 5

Level 1: Stories for Sight Word Comprehension 9

    My School 11

    I Like Hats 19

    It's Time to Go 27

    What Is in My Box? 35

    Jelly Beans 43

    How Many Cookies? 51

    The Park 59

    What Will I Do Tomorrow? 67

    Where Am I? 75

    I Draw 83

Level 2: Stories and Activities to Teach Comprehension Strategies 91

    The Birthday Party 92

    The Camping Trip 100

    Riding a Bike 108

    The Ice-Cream Store 116

    The Doghouse 124

    The Beach 132

    The Pet Store 140

    The Parade 148

    Grandma's House 156

    The Zoo 164

Sight Word Comprehension Cards List 172

Symbols/Sight Words Reference Chart 174

References 180

Introduction

Cindy is a third grade girl with autism. She amazed her family when she began to "read" at age 2 with no formal instruction. By third grade, she could read aloud almost any text put in front of her, and often read portions of the newspaper to her father. But unfortunately, Cindy was unable to answer questions about what she had read or to retell a simple story.

Does Cindy sound familiar to you? Cindy has a form of autism and is also hyperlexic. Many children with autism display symptoms of hyperlexia. *Hyperlexia* is defined as "the precocious self-taught ability to read words with an apparent lack of comprehension" (Mirenda and Erickson 2000, p. 349). Characteristics of hyperlexia include:

- word recognition skills that go beyond cognitive and/or language abilities
- compulsive reading of words
- being able to read at the age of 2-5
- being able to read without direct instruction (Silberberg & Silberberg 1967)
- a discrepancy between word recognition skills and reading comprehension   (Cobrinik 1974)

Some researchers are pointing to the link between language comprehension and reading comprehension. People with poor receptive language skills have more trouble comprehending what they have read than people with strong receptive language skills (Cunningham 1993). For children with autism, the weakness of their receptive language skills combines with their strength as visual learners to create hyperlexia (Mirenda & Erickson 2000).

How do we strengthen the comprehension of children with hyperlexia? First we want to look at what good young readers do. Good readers have broad background knowledge and vocabularies. Good readers use visual images to understand events, settings, and characters in the text. Good readers read words accurately and fluently, understanding the meaning of the words, phrases, and sentences as they read.

Many children with autism also read words accurately and fluently, yet they lack the background knowledge and understanding of vocabulary to attach meaning to the text. Children with autism often rely on visual information to understand the world around them. Our goal is to maximize the combined strengths of word recognition and visual learning to increase the comprehension of words and text for children with hyperlexia.

Poor readers "are often not familiar with the vocabulary they encounter and have trouble determining word meanings" (Texas Education Agency 2000). Children with autism also have trouble determining the meaning of words that they read. This is one of the hallmark features of hyperlexia. "For poor readers, comprehension can be enhanced through instruction focused on concept and vocabulary growth and background knowledge . . ." (Committee on the Prevention of Reading Difficulties in Young Children 1998). The strategies included in this kit will increase sight word vocabulary and help children with autism increase their comprehension of the words that they read.

All children need some instruction in reading comprehension, but it is critical for children with autism. In addition, children with autism need help creating visual images for words and sentences that they read. Typically developing children gain some comprehension from pictures before actual reading. Readers will often look at the cover of a book and predict what might happen in the book. As children become good readers, they tend to comprehend phrases and sentences (Calkins 2001). Children with hyperlexia can learn to comprehend at the word level (Frith and Snowling 1983) but are unable to make the mental images needed at both the word and sentence levels to become good readers.

For children with autism, the most important comprehension skill to develop is creating visual images. This kit not only aids them in creating visual images but also provides strategies for teaching more difficult comprehension skills.

The Basic Reading Comprehension Kit for Hyperlexia and Autism consists of two books and 578 sight word comprehension cards.

Storybook

This book consists of two levels. Level 1 has 10 simple stories using many of the sight words included in the Sight Word Comprehension Cards set. These stories serve as an introduction to teaching sight word vocabulary comprehension. Level 2 contains 10 more complex stories to help children with autism create visual images and practice important comprehension skills.

Level 1: Stories for Sight Word Comprehension

First, choose one of the stories (e.g., *My School*). Find the targeted Sight Word Comprehension Cards for the words used in the story. The targeted sight words are listed on the title page of each story. In *My School*, the words targeted are: *read, write, sing, color, play, work, fun, school, at*, and *have*. Begin by teaching four to six concepts at a time, although some children will be able to learn at a quicker rate. Keep in mind each child's skill and attention level when choosing the number of sight word concepts to teach at one time. (See the information on pages 7 and 8 for an explanation on how to use the Sight Word Comprehension Cards.)

After introducing the sight word concepts, read the story to the child. Let the child read the story to you. Emphasize the rhythm of the text. Try acting out the text with the child. Have fun! You may reproduce the stories for children to color and take home. Reread the new story often. Children love to revisit favorite stories.

Level 2: Stories and Activities to Teach Comprehension Strategies

Each story in this section provides opportunities to practice the following comprehension strategies:

- looking for details in a picture
- creating visual images of vocabulary words
- creating visual images of sentences
- finding specific information in a text
- sequencing events in a story
- finding the main idea

The activity pages with each story may be used in two ways: you may photocopy, color, and laminate the pages and cut-out cards to create a reusable set of activities for each story or you may photocopy the pages and have each student read, color, cut, and glue his or her own work.

Choose a story from Level 2.

1. Start with Page A. Look at the picture with the child. Point to the small pictures at the bottom of the page. Have the child circle each small picture that appears in the large picture. The child also may put an X on small pictures not found in the large picture. Then ask the *yes/no* questions. Some children will need to use the *yes/no* symbols to answer the questions.

2. Page B is a one-page story with picture symbols above the targeted vocabulary. Read the story to the child. Point to the picture symbols as you read.

3. Pages C and D help the child make a visual image for each sentence. As you read each sentence, use a blank sheet of paper to cover the unread sentences. Allow plenty of time for the child to process each sentence and picture. Page D gives additional practice in linking the sentence to a visual image. Have the child place each picture from page DD by the appropriate sentence.

4. Page E teaches children to answer *wh*-questions by finding details in the text. Read the sentence as you point to the picture prompt. Then read the question and point to the question picture prompt. Repeat the sentence and point to the picture prompt that answers the question. Read the question again and encourage the child to point to the picture prompt that answers the question.

5. Page F focuses on sequencing events in a story. The child should place the pictures above the first, next, and last symbols at the top of the page to represent three parts of the story.

6. Page G helps the child find the main idea of the story by choosing the best picture for the story and then choosing the title that matches the picture.

Dictionary
Good readers organize new words by connecting them to previously learned words or ideas for future retrieval. Children with autism lack the ability to organize new information with existing knowledge. Each word in the dictionary can be looked up for the meaning (in text) and/or for the category (in picture format). The definitions and sample sentences will help the child attach meaning to the word. By placing the dictionary pictures into categories, we are hoping to create a "semantic organizer" (Twachtman 1995, p. 147) to help children with autism organize new vocabulary and concepts.

Sight Word Comprehension Cards
These cards are a collection of 288 words commonly found in books for young readers. This list is adapted from a list found in *The Reading Teacher's Book of Lists* (Fry, Kress & Fountoukidis 2000). We have also included sight words that are not in our stories but are in many children's books so that the cards may be used with any children's literature.

Each sight word is printed in two ways: cards with text only and cards with a picture symbol on one side. Some cards may also have an illustration on the other side to provide different examples of the sight word. A complete listing of the Sight Word Comprehension Cards is on pages 172 – 173, and a reference chart matching the symbol with its sight word is on pages 174 – 179.

The Sight Word Comprehension Cards can be found in the eight booklets of perforated cards. Before you begin, carefully perforate the cards in each booklet. Match each sight word with its symbol and paper clip them together. Place each set of cards in an envelope (e.g., Pronouns, Words that Describe).

Introduce the concepts by using the cards with the pictures. Say the word aloud as you point to the picture. Next, place the cards in front of the child in a row. Say each picture and ask the child to point to the picture named. Give the child a card that has only the text on it. Read the word. Encourage the child to match the text card to the picture card.

The goals for students using the Sight Word Comprehension Cards are:

1. Identify picture symbols on the prompt cards.
2. Match text card to corresponding picture prompt card.
3. Read words in simple stories.

Few things are more rewarding to a teacher than helping a student understand a concept for the first time. We like to call this an "Aha!" It is our hope that as you use the materials in this kit, you will see the sparkle of understanding in a child's eyes. Learning to read is a gift for every child. We wish you all the best in your endeavor to give children the gift of reading.

Pam and Nena

Level 1

Stories for
Sight Word Comprehension

My
School

Targeted Sight Word Comprehension Words

at	play	sing
color	read	work
fun	school	write
have		

I   read   at   school.

I write at school.

I sing at school.

I   color   at   school.

I   play   at   school.

I   work   at   school.

I   have   fun   at   school.

I Like Hats

Targeted Sight Word Comprehension Words		
big	little	short
clean	new	soft
dirty	old	tall
hard	pretty	ugly

Hats,   hats,   I   like   hats!

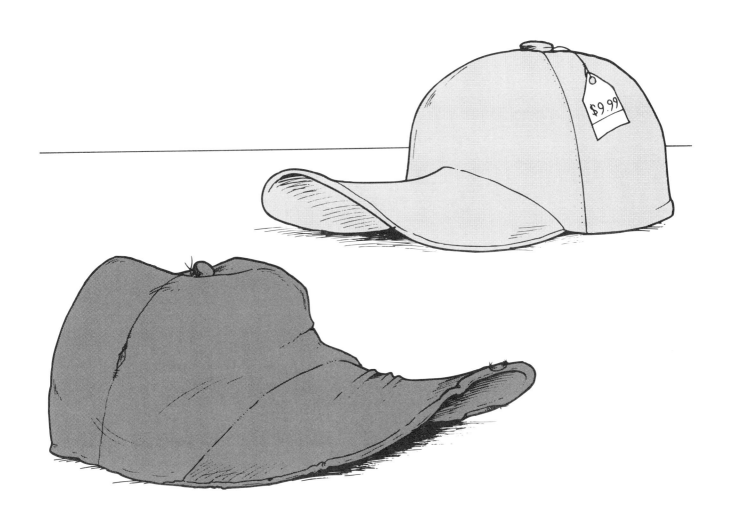

Old hat, new hat,

I like hats!

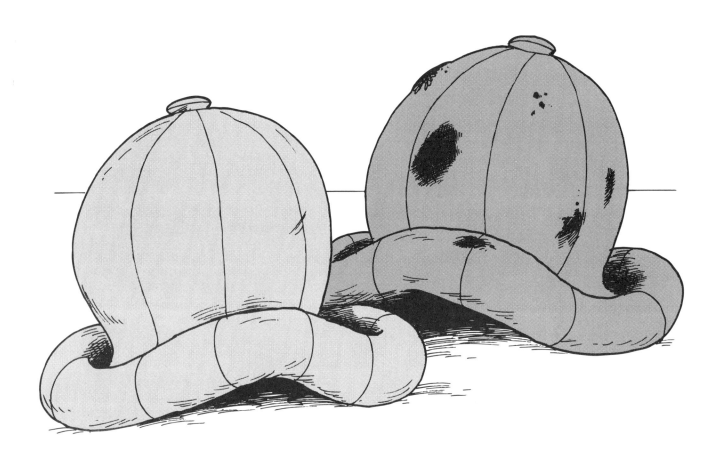

Clean hat, dirty hat,

I like hats!

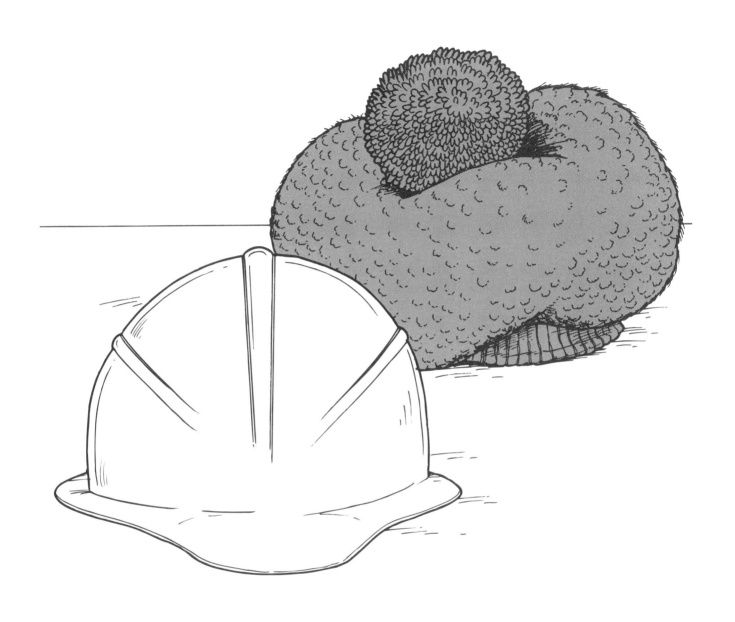

Hard hat, soft hat,

I like hats!

Tall hat, short hat,

I like hats!

 Pretty hat, ugly hat,

 I like hats!

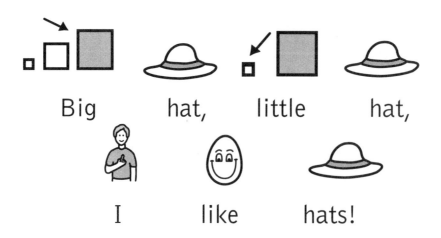

Big hat, little hat,

I like hats!

It's Time to Go

Targeted Sight Word Comprehension Words		
brother	go	mother
can	got	my
father	in	sister
friend		

My   father   got   in.

My   mother   got   in.

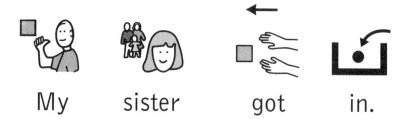

My   sister   got   in.

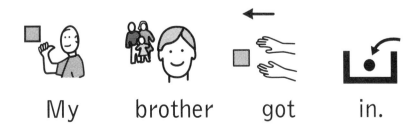

My   brother   got   in.

My   friend   got   in.

∧  →

Can I go?

Yes,   it's   time   to   go!

What Is in My Box?

Targeted Sight Word Comprehension Words

ball	coat	it
book	dog	new
box	hat	what
car	is	

What   is   in   my   box?

  a

Is it a new hat?

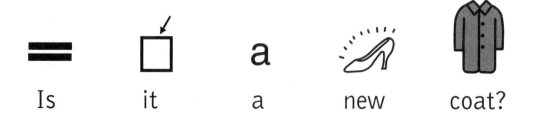

Is   it   a   new   coat?

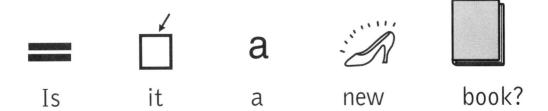

Is   it   a   new   book?

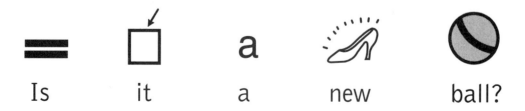

Is   it   a   new   ball?

 Is  it a a new car?

It's   a   new   dog!

Jelly Beans*

Targeted Sight Word Comprehension Words

are	purple	them
black	red	white
blue	so	yellow
green	some	

* Story can be sung to the tune of "The Farmer in the Dell."

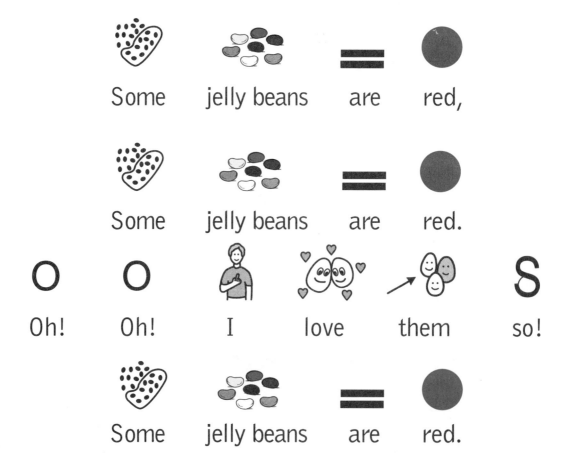

Some jelly beans are red,

Some jelly beans are red.

Oh! Oh! I love them so!

Some jelly beans are red.

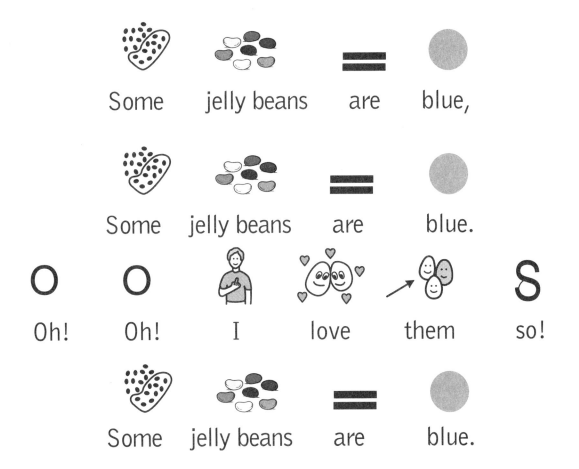

Some jelly beans are blue,

Some jelly beans are blue.

O Oh! O Oh! I love them so! S

Some jelly beans are blue.

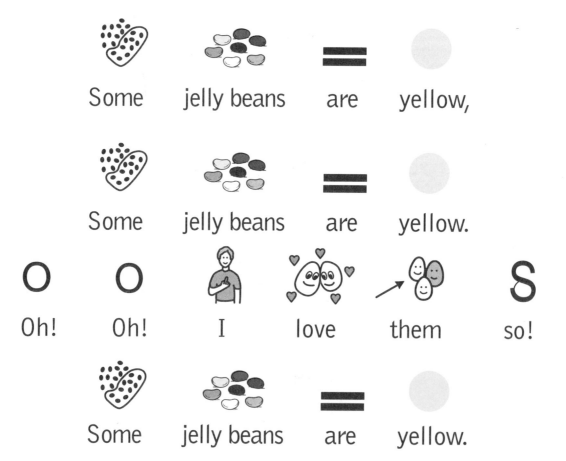

Some jelly beans are yellow,

Some jelly beans are yellow.

Oh! Oh! I love them so!

Some jelly beans are yellow.

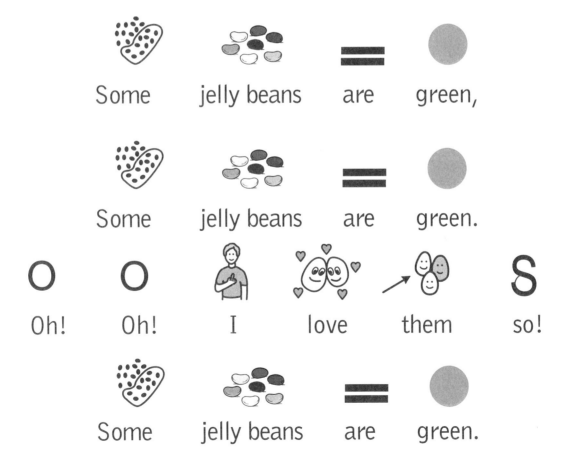

Some jelly beans are green,

Some jelly beans are green.

Oh! Oh! I love them so!

Some jelly beans are green.

  = ⬤

Some   jelly beans   are   purple,

  = ⬤

Some   jelly beans   are   purple.

O   O   S

Oh!   Oh!   I   love   them   so!

  = ⬤

Some   jelly beans   are   purple.

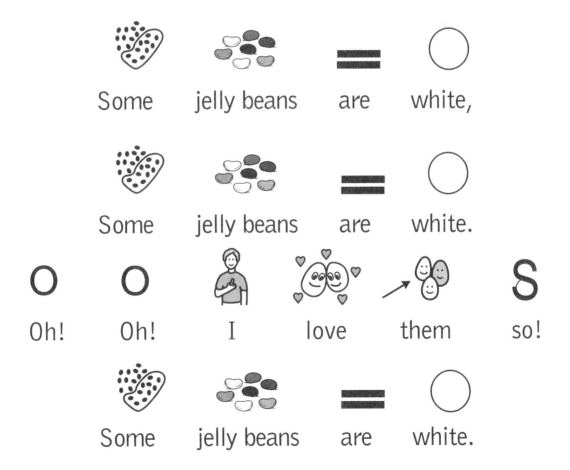

Some   jelly beans   =   white,

Some   jelly beans   =   white.

O   O   I   love   them   so!
Oh!   Oh!

Some   jelly beans   =   white.

  =

Some   jelly beans   are   black,

  =

Some   jelly beans   are   black.

O   O   ♥♥♥   S

Oh!   Oh!   I   love   them   so!

  =

Some   jelly beans   are   black.

How Many Cookies?

Targeted Sight Word Comprehension Words		
do	how	three
four	many	two
five	one	zero
have	six	

How many cookies do I have?

1

One

How many   cookies   do   I   have?

2

Two

How many   cookies   do   I   have?

3

Three

How many cookies do I have?

4

Four

How many cookies do I have?

5

Five

How many cookies do I have?

6

Six

How many cookies do I have?

0

Zero!

The Park

Targeted Sight Word Comprehension Words

find	so	up
high	sit	walk
jump	swing	water
run		

Run,   run   to   the   park.

Jog,   jog,   jog.

Swing, swing   up   so   high.

Pump, pump, pump.

The Park

Basic Reading Comprehension Kit   61

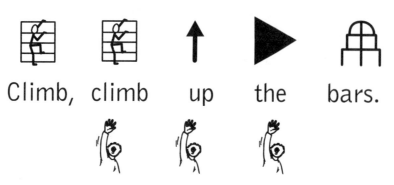

Climb, climb   up   the   bars.

Reach, reach, reach.

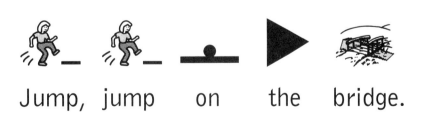

Jump, jump   on   the   bridge.

Wobble, wobble, wobble.

Hide,   hide,   hide   +   and   seek.

Find,   find,   find.

Walk,   walk   to   the   water.

Drink,   drink,   drink.

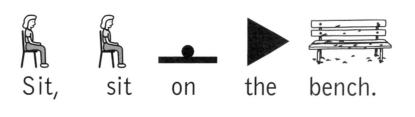

Sit,   sit   on   the   bench.

Rest,   rest,   rest.

The Park
Basic Reading Comprehension Kit   66

What Will I Do Tomorrow?

Targeted Sight Word Comprehension Words

do	where	why
how	which	will
what	who	with
when		

What   will   I   do   tomorrow?

Go   swimming.

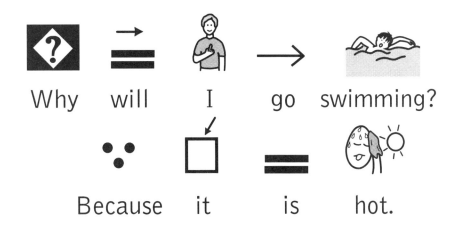

Why will I go swimming?

Because it is hot.

When   will   I   go   swimming?

      1

At   1   o'clock.

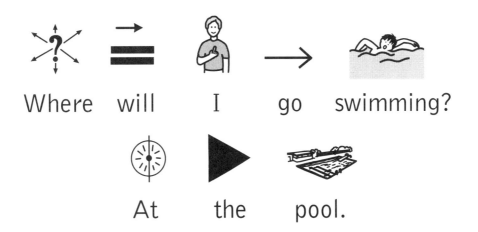

Where will I go swimming?

At the pool.

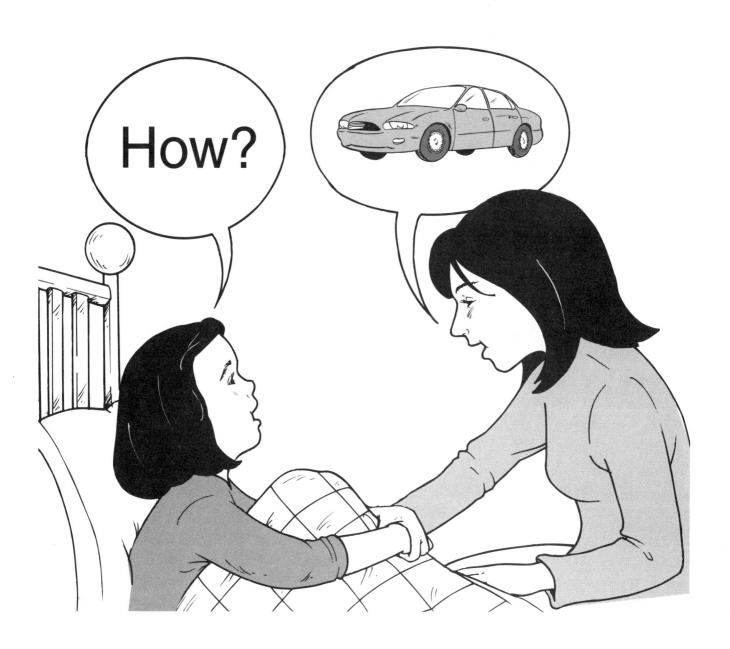

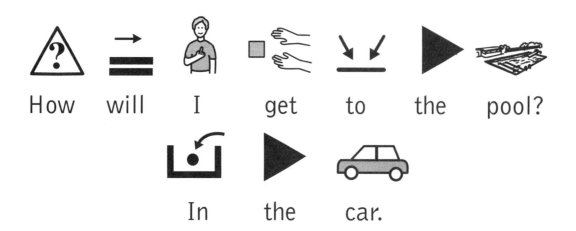

How will I get to the pool?

In the car.

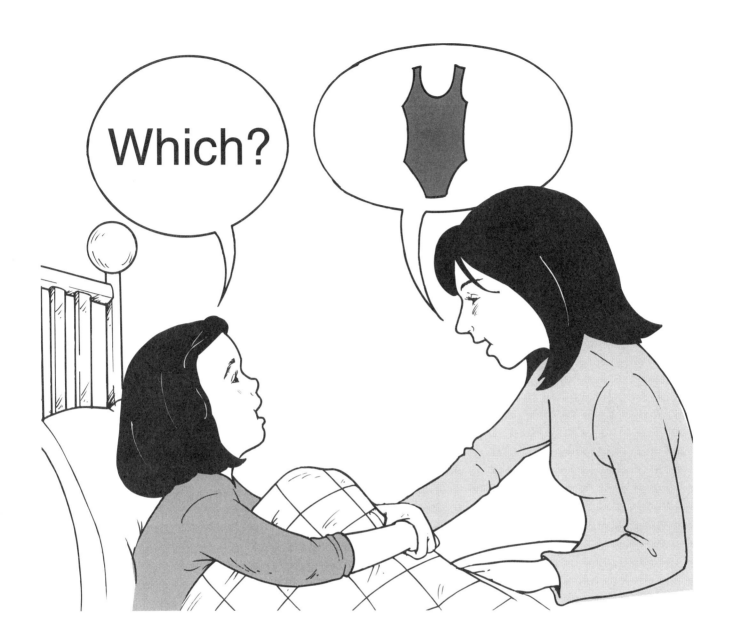

Which   swimsuit   will   I   wear?

        1

The   red   one.

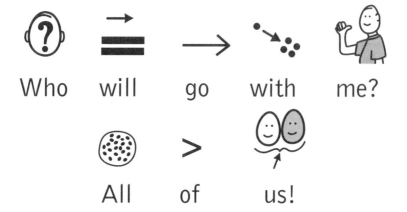

Who will go with me?

All of us!

Where Am I?

Targeted Sight Word Comprehension Words		
am	eyes	under
by	in	where
close	on	your
clothes		

under

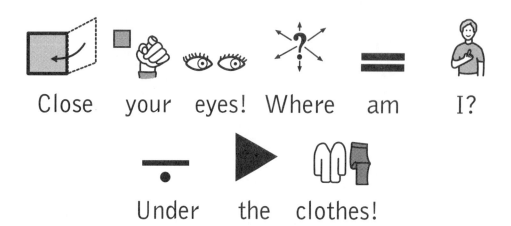

Close your eyes! Where am I?

Under the clothes!

on

Close   your   eyes!   Where   am   I?

On   the   stairs!

behind

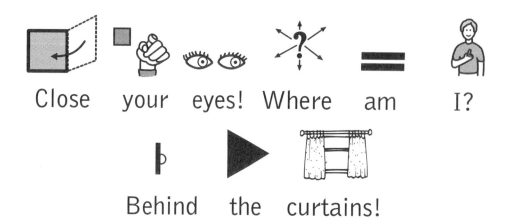

Close your eyes! Where am I?

Behind the curtains!

by

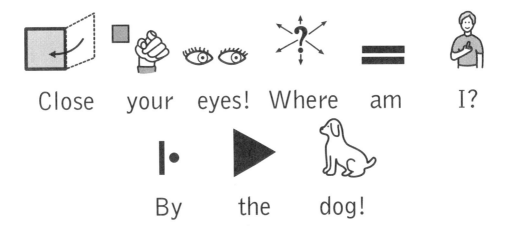

Close your eyes! Where am I?

By the dog!

beside

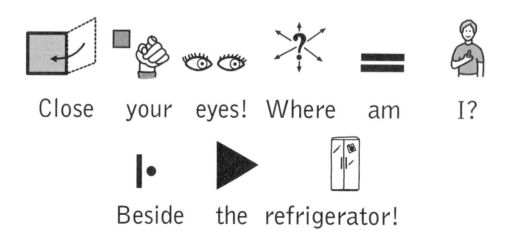

Close your eyes! Where am I?

Beside the refrigerator!

between

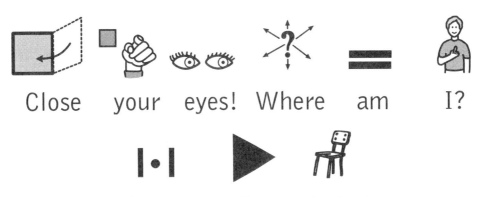

Close your eyes! Where am I?

Between the chairs!

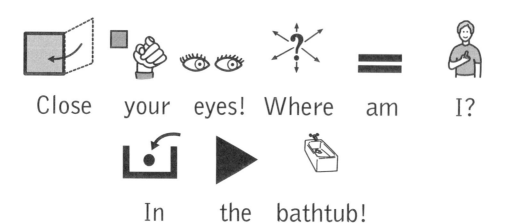

Close your eyes! Where am I?

In the bathtub!

I Draw

Targeted Sight Word Comprehension Words		
draw	hair	me
ears	head	mouth
eyes	it	nose

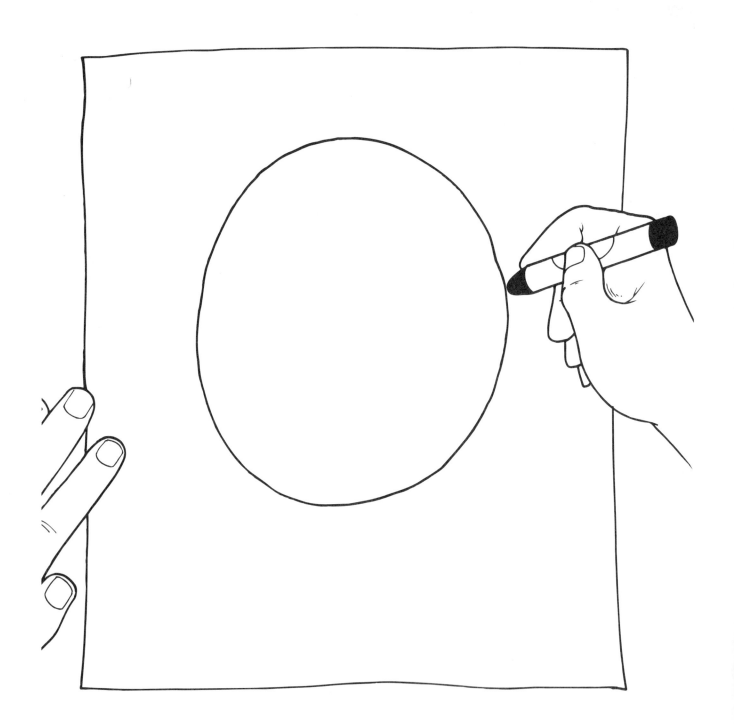

I   draw   the   head.

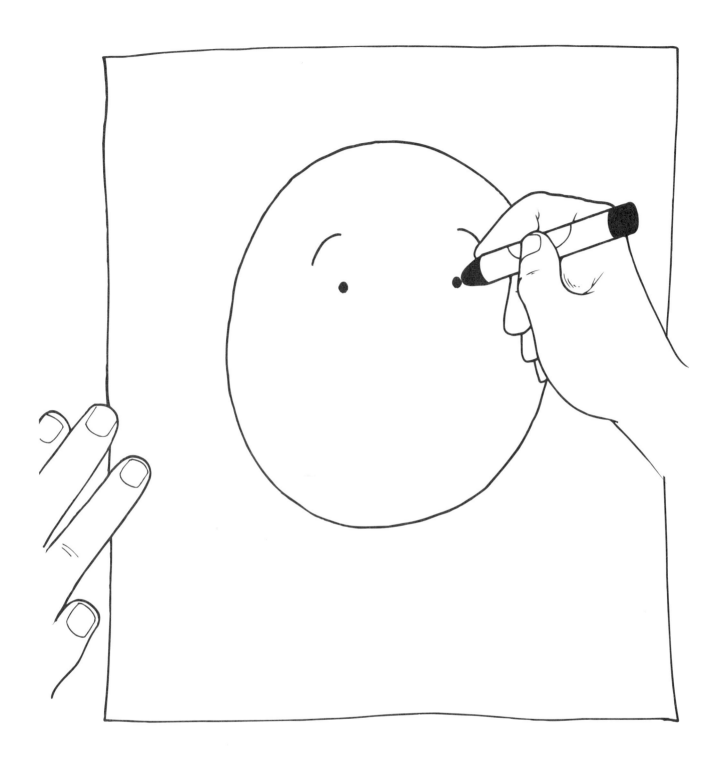

I　　draw　　the　　eyes.

I   draw   the   nose.

I   draw   the   mouth.

I   draw   the   ears.

I   draw   the   hair.

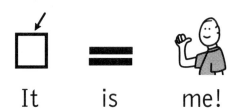

It   is   me!

Level 2

Stories and Activities
to Teach
Comprehension Strategies

Note: The symbol for last *on pages 98, 106, 114, 122, 130, 138, 146, 154, 162, and 170 is different from the symbol for* last *on the Sight Word Comprehension Cards. This is because there are only three pictures to sequence in the activity on those pages and we wanted to keep it simple by using* ↓ 1 2 3 *instead of* 1 2 3 4 ↓ *. Having different symbols or pictures for the same word can teach generalization to students. It helps them learn that there are different ways to look at things, and that different situations may require different symbols or pictures to best represent the idea.*

The Birthday Party: Looking for Details in a Picture

Is there a cake?
Are there balloons?
Do you see presents?
Is the girl sitting down?
Do the boys have on hats?

Yes	No

Circle things you see in the picture. Put an X on things that are not in the picture.

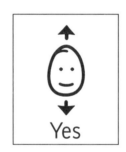

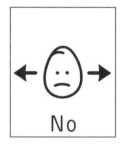

The Birthday Party: Vocabulary Expansion

Today is Brett's birthday.

Brett will have a party.

Rosa and Marcus will go to the party.

Rosa and Marcus will bring presents.

Brett will open the presents.

Everyone will have fun at the party.

The Birthday Party: Making Visual Images Part 1

Today is Brett's birthday.

Brett will have a party.

Rosa and Marcus will go to the party.

Rosa and Marcus will bring presents.

Brett will open the presents.

Everyone will have fun at the party.

The Birthday Party: Making Visual Images Part 2

Read each sentence. Find the picture on page 96 that matches and place it in the box beside the sentence.

Today is Brett's birthday.

Brett will have a party.

Rosa and Marcus will go to the party.

Rosa and Marcus will bring presents.

Brett will open the presents.

Everyone will have fun at the party.

Cut apart the pictures.   Match each picture to the right sentence on page 95.

The Birthday Party: Looking for Details

 Today is Brett's birthday.

 When is Brett's birthday?

 Brett will have a party.

 What will Brett have?

 Rosa and Marcus will go to the party.

 Where will Rosa and Marcus go?

 Rosa and Marcus will bring presents.

 Who will bring presents?

 Brett will open the presents.

 What will Brett open?

 Everyone will have fun at the party.

 Who will have fun at the party?

The Birthday Party: Sequencing Events

Cut apart the pictures. Then place the pictures in the correct order.

First	Next	Last
↓		↓
1 2 3		**1 2 3**

The Birthday Party: **Main Idea**

Today is Brett's birthday. Brett will have a party. Rosa and Marcus will go to the party. Rosa and Marcus will bring presents. Brett will open the presents. Everyone will have fun at the party.

Which picture matches the story?

A title is a name for a story. Which title matches the story?

1. Brett Has a Dog
2. Brett's Birthday Party
3. Brett Is Sick

The Camping Trip: Looking for Details in a Picture

Are people fishing?
Do you see a tent?
Is there a house?
Is there a fire?
Do they have bicycles?

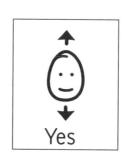 Yes

 No

---

Circle things you see in the picture. Put an X on things that are not in the picture.

The Camping Trip: Vocabulary Expansion

Maria and Carlos go camping with their family.

Carlos helps Dad put up the tent.

They all go fishing.

Maria and Mom make a fire.

Mom and Dad cook the fish for dinner.

At night, the family sleeps in the tent.

The Camping Trip: Making Visual Images Part 1

Maria and Carlos go camping with their family.

Carlos helps Dad put up the tent.

They all go fishing.

Maria and Mom make a fire.

Mom and Dad cook the fish for dinner.

At night, the family sleeps in the tent.

Read each sentence. Find the picture on page 104 that matches and place it in the box beside the sentence.

Maria and Carlos go camping with their family.

Carlos helps Dad put up the tent.

They all go fishing.

Maria and Mom make a fire.

Mom and Dad cook the fish for dinner.

At night, the family sleeps in the tent.

Cut apart the pictures. Match each picture to the right sentence on page 103.

The Camping Trip: Looking for Details

Maria and Carlos go camping with their family. *Where do Maria and Carlos go?*

Carlos helps Dad put up the tent. *Who helps Dad put up the tent?*

They all go fishing. *Where do they all go?*

Maria and Mom make a fire. *What do Maria and Mom make?*

Mom and Dad cook the fish for dinner. *Why do Mom and Dad cook the fish?*

At night, the family sleeps in the tent. *When does the family sleep in the tent?*

The Camping Trip: Sequencing Events

Cut apart the pictures. Then place the pictures in the correct order.

First	Next	Last

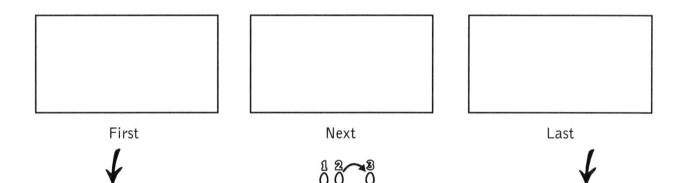

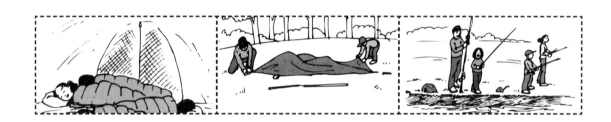

The Camping Trip: Main Idea

Maria and Carlos go camping with their family. Carlos helps Dad put up the tent. They all go fishing. Maria and Mom make a fire. Mom and Dad cook the fish for dinner. At night, the family sleeps in the tent.

Which picture matches the story?

A title is a name for a story. Which title matches the story?

1. Maria and Carlos Go to the Circus
2. Fish Live in the Ocean
3. Maria and Carlos Go Camping

Riding a Bike: Looking for Details in a Picture

Do you see a bike?

Is there a girl?

Is there a dog?

Is the girl riding a horse?

Is Dad helping the girl?

Yes

No

Circle things you see in the picture.   Put an X on things that are not in the picture.

Riding a Bike: Vocabulary Expansion

Yesterday Emily tried to ride her bike.

Oh, no! The bike fell over.

Emily asked Dad for help.

Dad pushed the bike.

Then Emily tried again.

Hurrah! Emily rode her bike!

Yesterday Emily tried to ride her bike.

Oh, no! The bike fell over.

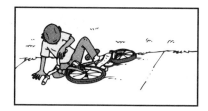

Emily asked Dad for help.

Dad pushed the bike.

Then Emily tried again.

Hurrah! Emily rode her bike!

Riding a Bike: Making Visual Images Part 2

Read each sentence. Find the picture on page 112 that matches and place it in the box beside the sentence.

Yesterday Emily tried to ride her bike.

Oh, no! The bike fell over.

Emily asked Dad for help.

Dad pushed the bike.

Then Emily tried again.

Hurrah! Emily rode her bike!

Cut apart the pictures. Match each picture to the right sentence on page 111.

Riding a Bike: Looking for Details

Yesterday Emily tried to ride her bike. *When did Emily try to ride her bike?*

Oh, no! The bike fell over. *What fell over?*

Emily asked Dad for help. *Who asked Dad for help?*

Dad pushed the bike. *What did Dad push?*

Then Emily tried again. *Who tried again?*

Hurrah! Emily rode her bike! *Why did Dad say "Hurrah"?*

Riding a Bike: Sequencing Events

Cut apart the pictures. Then place the pictures in the correct order.

First   Next   Last

1 2 3   **1 2 3**

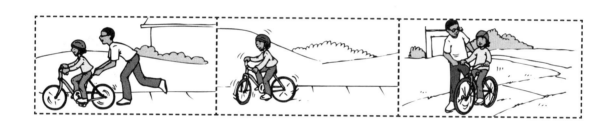

Riding a Bike: Main Idea

Yesterday Emily tried to ride her bike. Oh, no! The bike fell over. Emily asked Dad for help. Dad pushed the bike. Then Emily tried again. Hurrah! Emily rode her bike!

Which picture matches the story?

A title is a name for a story. Choose the best title for the story.

1. Emily Learns to Ride a Bike
2. Emily Sails a Boat
3. Emily Takes a Walk

The Ice-Cream Store: Looking For Details in a Picture

Do you see an ice-cream cone?
Do you see a hot dog?
Is there a couch?
Are the children at the zoo?
Are the children happy?

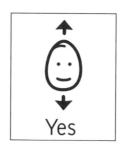

Yes

No

Circle things you see in the picture. Put an X on things that are not in the picture.

James and his friends wanted ice cream.

They went to the ice-cream store.

Keesha got a chocolate ice-cream cone.

Lucas got a strawberry milkshake.

James got a banana split.

They ate treats on a hot summer day.

117

James and his friends wanted ice cream.

They went to the ice-cream store.

Keesha got a chocolate ice-cream cone.

Lucas got a strawberry milkshake.

James got a banana split.

They ate treats on a hot summer day.

The Ice-Cream Store: Making Visual Images Part 2

Read each sentence. Find the picture on page 120 that matches and place it in the box beside the sentence.

James and his friends wanted ice cream.

They went to the ice-cream store.

Keesha got a chocolate ice-cream cone.

Lucas got a strawberry milkshake.

James got a banana split.

They ate treats on a hot summer day.

Cut apart the pictures. Match each picture to the right sentence on page 119.

The Ice-Cream Store: Looking for Details

James and his friends wanted ice cream. *What did James and his friends want?*

They went to the ice-cream store. *Where did they go?*

Keesha got a chocolate ice-cream cone. *Who got a chocolate ice-cream cone?*

Lucas got a strawberry milkshake. *What kind of milkshake did Lucas get?*

James got a banana split. *Who got a banana split?*

They ate treats on a hot summer day. *What did they eat on a hot summer day?*

The Ice-Cream Store: Sequencing Events

Cut apart the pictures. Then place the pictures in the correct order.

First	Next	Last

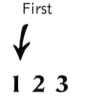

The Ice-Cream Store: Main Idea

James and his friends wanted ice cream. They went to the ice-cream store. Keesha got a chocolate ice-cream cone. Lucas got a strawberry milkshake. James got a banana split. They ate treats on a hot summer day.

Which picture matches the story?

A title is a name for a story. Choose the best title for the story.

1. Going to the Ice-Cream Store
2. James Plays Baseball
3. Going to the Pizza Store

The Doghouse: Looking for Details in a Picture

Do you see a refrigerator?
Do you see a dog?
Is there a hammer?
Are the people eating?
Are they inside the house?

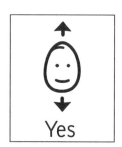

Yes

No

Circle things you see in the picture. Put an X on things that are not in the picture.

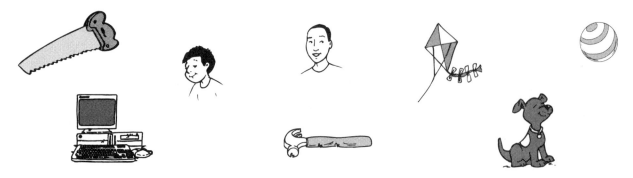

The Doghouse: Vocabulary Expansion

Jeff and his dad built a doghouse for Spot.

They needed wood, tools, and nails.

They measured and cut the wood for the walls.

Dad helped Jeff hammer the nails.

They worked all day.

Spot liked his new doghouse.

Jeff and his dad built a doghouse for Spot.

They needed wood, tools, and nails.

They measured and cut the wood for the walls.

Dad helped Jeff hammer the nails.

They worked all day.

Spot liked his new doghouse.

Read each sentence. Find the picture on page 128 that matches and place it in the box beside the sentence.

Jeff and his dad built a doghouse for Spot.

They needed wood, tools, and nails.

They measured and cut the wood for the walls.

Dad helped Jeff hammer the nails.

They worked all day.

Spot liked his new doghouse.

Cut apart the pictures. Match each picture to the right sentence on page 127.

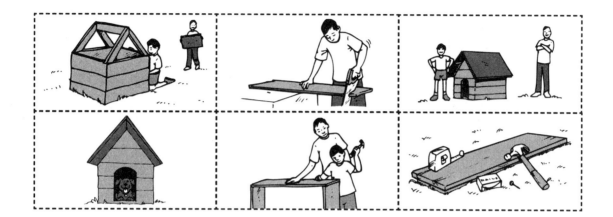

The Doghouse: Looking for Details

Jeff and his dad built a doghouse for Spot. *Who built a doghouse for Spot?*

They needed wood, tools, and nails. *What did they need?*

They measured and cut the wood for the walls. *What did they measure and cut?*

Dad helped Jeff hammer the nails. *Who helped Jeff hammer the nails?*

They worked all day. *How long did they work?*

Spot liked his new doghouse. *What did Spot like?*

The Doghouse: Sequencing Events

Cut apart the pictures. Then place the pictures in the correct order.

First

Next

Last

1 2 3

1 2 3

The Doghouse: Main Idea

Jeff and his dad built a doghouse for Spot. They needed wood,

tools, and nails. They measured and cut the wood for the walls.

Dad helped Jeff hammer the nails. They worked all day. Spot

liked his new doghouse.

Which picture matches the story?

A title is a name for a story. Choose the best title for the story.

1. Dogs Are Good Pets
2. Building a New Doghouse
3. Jeff Climbs a Tree

The Beach: Looking for Details in a Picture

Do you see a slide?
Do you see water?
Is there an umbrella?
Are people swimming?
Is it cold outside?

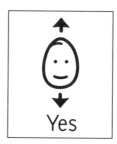
Yes

No

Circle things you see in the picture. Put an X on things that are not in the picture.

Basic Reading Comprehension Kit

The Beach: Vocabulary Expansion

Last summer Julie went to the beach.

Julie went to the beach in an airplane.

She played in the sand.

She swam in the water.

Julie looked for seashells.

Julie found a starfish!

Last summer Julie went to the beach.

Julie went to the beach in an airplane.

She played in the sand.

She swam in the water.

Julie looked for seashells.

Julie found a starfish!

The Beach: Making Visual Images Part 2

Read each sentence. Find the picture on page 136 that matches and place it in the box beside the sentence.

Last summer Julie went to the beach.

Julie went to the beach in an airplane.

She played in the sand.

She swam in the water.

Julie looked for seashells.

Julie found a starfish!

Cut apart the pictures. Match each picture to the right sentence on page 135.

The Beach: Looking for Details

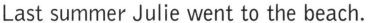

Last summer Julie went to the beach.

When did Julie go to the beach?

Julie went to the beach in an airplane.

How did Julie go to the beach?

She played in the sand.

Where did she play?

She swam in the water.

What did Julie do in the water?

Julie looked for seashells.

Who looked for seashells?

Julie found a starfish!

What did Julie find?

The Beach: Sequencing Events

Cut apart the pictures.   Then place the pictures in the correct order.

First   Next   Last

The Beach: Main Idea

Last summer, Julie went to the beach. Julie went to the beach in an airplane. She played in the sand. She swam in the water. Julie looked for seashells. Julie found a starfish!

Which picture matches the story?

A title is a name for a story. Choose the best title for the story.

1. Julie Goes to School
2. Julie Goes Shopping
3. Julie Goes to the Beach

The Pet Store: Looking for Details in a Picture

Do you see a rabbit?
Do you see a horse?
Is there a bird?
Is the boy holding a snake?
Is the boy's mom with him?

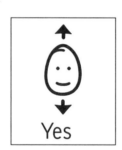

Yes

No

Circle things you see in the picture. Put an X on things that are not in the picture.

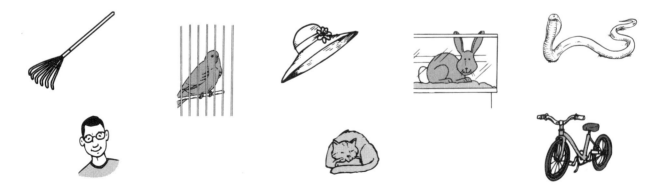

The Pet Store: Vocabulary Expansion

Sam wanted a new pet.

Dad took him to the pet store.

"Do you want a bird?" "No," said Sam.

"Do you want a rabbit?" "No," said Sam.

"Do you want a puppy?" "Yes!" said Sam.

Sam loves his new puppy.

The Pet Store: Making Visual Images Part 1

Sam wanted a new pet.

Dad took him to the pet store.

"Do you want a bird?" "No," said Sam.

"Do you want a rabbit?" "No," said Sam.

"Do you want a puppy?" "Yes!" said Sam.

Sam loves his new puppy.

The Pet Store: Making Visual Images Part 2

Read each sentence. Find the picture on page 144 that matches and place it in the box beside the sentence.

Sam wanted a new pet.

Dad took him to the pet store.

"Do you want a bird?" "No," said Sam.

"Do you want a rabbit?" "No," said Sam.

"Do you want a puppy?" "Yes!" said Sam.

Sam loves his new puppy.

Cut apart the pictures. Match each picture to the right sentence on page 143.

The Pet Store: Looking for Details

Sam wanted a new pet. *Who wanted a new pet?*

Dad took him to the pet store. *Where did Dad take Sam?*

"Do you want a bird?" "No," said Sam. *What did Sam say?*

"Do you want a rabbit?" "No," said Sam. *What did Sam say?*

"Do you want a puppy?" "Yes!" said Sam. *What did Sam say?*

Sam loves his new puppy. *Who loves the new puppy?*

The Pet Store: Sequencing Events

Cut apart the pictures. Then place the pictures in the correct order.

First   Next   Last

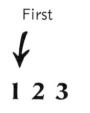

1 2 3

1 2 3

The Pet Store: Main Idea

Sam wanted a new pet. Dad took him to the pet store.

"Do you want a bird?" "No," said Sam.

"Do you want a rabbit?" "No," said Sam.

"Do you want a puppy?" "Yes!" said Sam.

Sam loves his new puppy.

Which picture matches the story?

A title is a name for a story. Choose the best title for the story.

1. Sam's New Teacher
2. Sam's New Coat
3. Sam's New Pet

The Parade: Looking for Details in a Picture

Do you see a clown?
Do you see a cow?
Is there a tractor?
Is there a drum?
Are people waving?

Yes

No

Circle things you see in the picture. Put an X on things that are not in the picture.

The Parade: Vocabulary Expansion

 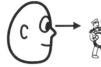

Kate watched a parade with her mom.

The band marched down the street.

The clown drove a funny car.

The fire engine made a loud noise.

People on a float waved at Kate.

Kate and her mom waved too.

The Parade: Making Visual Images Part 1

Kate watched a parade with her mom.

The band marched down the street.

The clown drove a funny car.

The fire engine made a loud noise.

People on a float waved at Kate.

Kate and her mom waved too.

The Parade: Making Visual Images Part 2

Read each sentence. Find the picture on page 152 that matches and place it in the box beside the sentence.

Kate watched a parade with her mom.

The band marched down the street.

The clown drove a funny car.

The fire engine made a loud noise.

People on a float waved at Kate.

Kate and her mom waved too.

Cut apart the pictures. Match each picture to the right sentence on page 151.

The Parade: Looking for Details

Kate watched a parade with her mom.   *Who watched a parade with Mom?*

The band marched down the street.   *Where did the band march?*

The clown drove a funny car.   *Who drove a funny car?*

The fire engine made a loud noise.   *What made a loud noise?*

People on a float waved at Kate.   *Where were the people?*

Kate and her mom waved too.   *What did Kate and her mom do?*

The Parade: Sequencing Events

Cut apart the pictures. Then place the pictures in the correct order.

First

1 2 3

Next

Last

1 2 3

The Parade: Main Idea

Kate watched a parade with her mom. The band marched down the street. The clown drove a funny car. The fire engine made a loud noise. People on a float waved at Kate. Kate and her mom waved too.

Which picture matches the story?

A title is a name for a story. Choose the best title for the story.

1. Kate and Mom See Fireworks
2. Kate and Mom Have a Race
3. Kate and Mom See a Parade

Grandma's House: Looking for Details in a Picture

Do you see a tire swing?
Do you see a monkey?
Is there a slide?
Is there a flag?
Is Grandma pushing the swing?

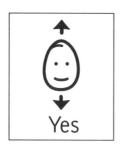

Yes

No

Circle things you see in the picture. Put an X on things that are not in the picture.

Grandma's House: Vocabulary Expansion

Matt went to visit his grandma.

Grandma and Matt had fun.

Grandma pushed Matt on the tire swing.

They played checkers and Matt won.

They ate cookies and drank milk.

At night, Grandma read a story to Matt.

Matt went to visit his grandma.

Grandma and Matt had fun.

Grandma pushed Matt on the tire swing.

They played checkers and Matt won.

They ate cookies and drank milk.

At night, Grandma read a story to Matt.

158

Grandma's House: Making Visual Images Part 2

Read each sentence. Find the picture on page 160 that matches and place it in the box beside the sentence.

Matt went to visit his grandma.

Grandma and Matt had fun.

Grandma pushed Matt on the tire swing.

They played checkers and Matt won.

They ate cookies and drank milk.

At night, Grandma read a story to Matt.

Cut apart the pictures. Match each picture to the right sentence on page 159.

Grandma's House: Looking for Details

Matt went to visit his grandma.   *Who did Matt visit?*

Grandma and Matt had fun.   *Who had fun?*

Grandma pushed Matt on the tire swing.   *Where was Matt?*

They played checkers and Matt won.   *What did they play?*

They ate cookies and drank milk.   *What did they drink?*

At night, Grandma read a story to Matt.   *When did Grandma read a story to Matt?*

Grandma's House: Sequencing Events

Cut apart the pictures. Then place the pictures in the correct order.

First

Next

Last

1 2 3

1 2 3

Grandma's House: Main Idea

Matt went to visit his grandma. Grandma and Matt had fun. Grandma pushed Matt on the tire swing. They played checkers and Matt won. They ate cookies and drank milk. At night, Grandma read a story to Matt.

Which picture matches the story?

A title is a name for a story. Choose the best title for the story.

1. Matt Visits the Farm
2. Matt Visits Grandma
3. Matt Plays the Guitar

The Zoo: Looking for Details in a Picture

Do you see a giraffe?
Do you see a fire truck?
Do you see a bus?
Is there a school?
Do you see a lion?

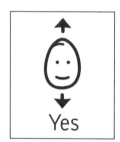

Circle things you see in the picture. Put an X on things that are not in the picture.

The Zoo: Vocabulary Expansion

Ryan and his friends are going to the zoo.

First they will see giraffes and zebras.

Next they will pet rabbits and goats.

Ryan likes lions the best.

After they see all the animals, they will eat lunch.

Then they will go back to school.

The Zoo: Making Visual Images Part 1

Ryan and his friends are going to the zoo.

First they will see giraffes and zebras.

Next they will pet rabbits and goats.

Ryan likes lions the best.

After they see all the animals, they will eat lunch.

Then they will go back to school.

The Zoo: Making Visual Images Part 2

Read each sentence. Find the picture on page 168 that matches and place it in the box beside the sentence.

Ryan and his friends are going to the zoo.

First they will see giraffes and zebras.

Next they will pet rabbits and goats.

Ryan likes lions the best.

After they see all the animals, they will eat lunch.

Then they will go back to school.

Cut apart the pictures. Match each picture to the right sentence on page 167.

The Zoo: Looking for Details

Ryan and his friends are going to the zoo. *Where is Ryan's class going?*

First they will see giraffes and zebras. *What will they see first?*

Next they will pet rabbits and goats. *What will they pet?*

Ryan likes lions the best. *Who likes lions best?*

After they see all the animals, they will eat lunch. *What will they eat?*

Then they will go back to school. *Where will they go?*

The Zoo: Sequencing Events

Cut apart the pictures. Then place the pictures in the correct order.

First   Next   Last

1 2 3   1 2 3

The Zoo: Main Idea

Ryan and his friends are going to the zoo. First they will see giraffes and zebras. Next they will pet rabbits and goats. Ryan likes lions the best. After they see all the animals, they will eat lunch. Then they will go back to school.

Which picture matches the story?

A title is a name for a story. Choose the best title for the story.

1. Ryan Goes to the Zoo
2. Ryan Goes on a Picnic
3. Ryan Calls his Grandma

Sight Word Comprehension Cards List

Functional Words
a
about
again
an
and
at
away
because
but
from
here
if
never
no
not
o'clock
of
once
or
please
so
soon
sure
then
there
to
until
while
with
yes

Words that Describe
all
another
best
better
big
both
clean
cold
dear

dirty
each
fast
fat
full
fun
funny
good
happy
hard
high
hot
kind
little
long
many
more
most
much
new
old
only
other
pretty
same
short
small
soft
some
tall
that
ugly
very
warm

Color Words
black
blue
brown
green
orange
purple

red
white
yellow

Words that Name
ball
bed
book
box
can
car
cat
clothes
coat
day
dog
door
drink
fish
fly
hat
home
house
morning
name
night
park
play
present
saw
school
show
swing
thing
tree
water
year

Body Parts
back
ear
eyes

foot
hair
hand
head
mouth
nose

People
boy
brother
father
friend
girl
man
men
mother
people
sister
woman
women

Pronouns
he
her
him
his
I
it
me
my
our
she
their
them
these
they
this
us
we
you
your

Doing Words

am	leave
are	let
ask	like
ate	live
be	look
bring	love
buy	made
call	make
came	open
can	play
clean	put
close	ran
color	read
come	ride
could	run
cut	said
did	sat
do	saw
draw	see
drink	should
eat	show
fall	sing
find	sit
fish	sleep
fly	stand
gave	start
get	stop
give	swim
go	swing
goes	take
got	tell
had	thank
has	think
have	took
hear	try
help	turn
hope	use
is	walk
jump	want
know	was
laugh	wash
	water

were
will
wish
work
would
write

Question Words

how
what
when
where
which
who
why

Sequence Words

after
before
eight
end
first
five
four
last
left
next
one
right
second
seven
six
ten
third
three
today

tomorrow
two
yesterday
zero

Position Words

around
back
by
down
far
in
into
near
off
on
out
over
under
up

Symbols/Sight Words Reference Chart

Functional Words

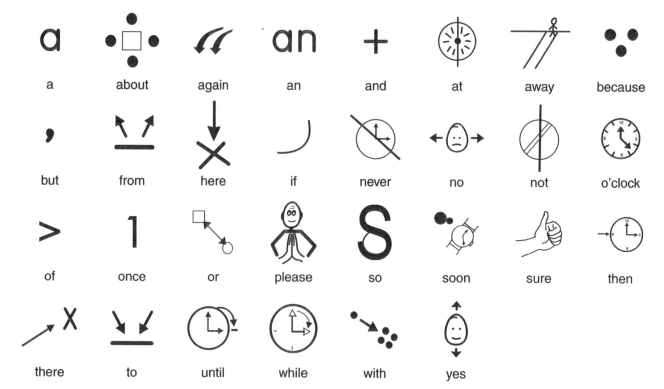

a	about	again	an	and	at	away	because
but	from	here	if	never	no	not	o'clock
of	once	or	please	so	soon	sure	then
there	to	until	while	with	yes		

Words that Describe

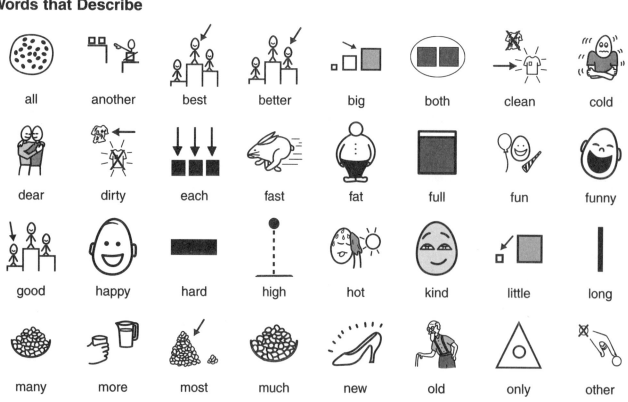

all	another	best	better	big	both	clean	cold
dear	dirty	each	fast	fat	full	fun	funny
good	happy	hard	high	hot	kind	little	long
many	more	most	much	new	old	only	other

Words that Describe, *continued*

pretty	same	short	small	soft	some

tall	that	ugly	very	warm

Color Words

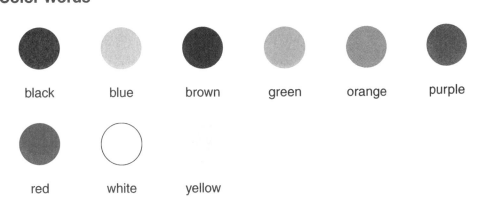

black	blue	brown	green	orange	purple

red	white	yellow

Words that Name

ball	bed	book	box	can	car	cat	clothes

coat	day	dog	door	drink	fish	fly	hat

home	house	morning	name	night	park	play	present

Words that Name, *continued*

saw	school	show	swing	thing	tree	water	year

Body Parts

back	ear	eyes	foot	hair

hand	head	mouth	nose

People

boy	brother	father	friend	girl	man

men	mother	people	sister	woman	women

Pronouns

he	her	him	his	I	it

me	my	our	she	their	them

Pronouns, *continued*

these	they	this	us	we	you	your

Doing Words

am	are	ask	ate	be	bring	buy	call

came	can	clean	close	color	come	could	cut

did	do	draw	drink	eat	fall	find	fish

fly	gave	get	give	go	goes	got	had

has	have	hear	help	hope	is	jump	know

laugh	leave	let	like	live	look	love	made

make	open	play	put	ran	read	ride	run

Doing Words, *continued*

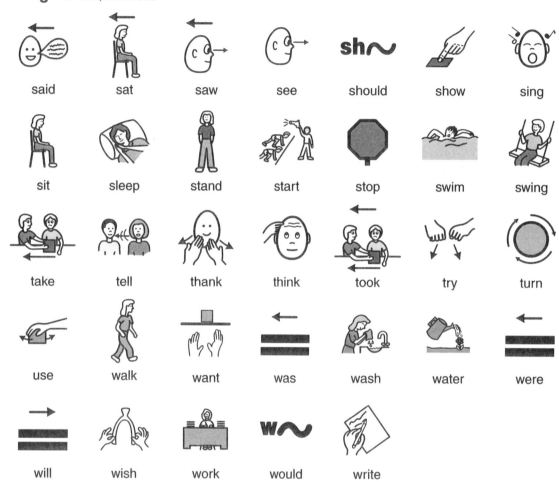

said	sat	saw	see	should	show	sing
sit	sleep	stand	start	stop	swim	swing
take	tell	thank	think	took	try	turn
use	walk	want	was	wash	water	were
will	wish	work	would	write		

Question Words

how	what	when	where	which	who	why

Sequence Words

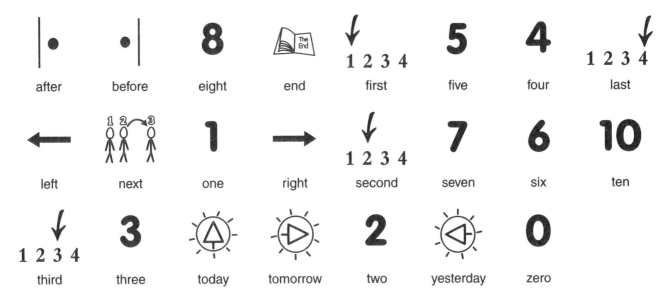

after   before   eight   end   first   five   four   last

left   next   one   right   second   seven   six   ten

third   three   today   tomorrow   two   yesterday   zero

Position Words

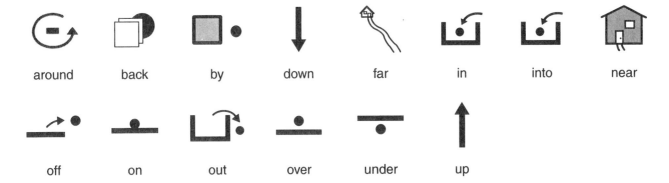

around   back   by   down   far   in   into   near

off   on   out   over   under   up

References

Calkins, L. M. (2001). *The art of teaching reading.* New York: Addison-Wesley Educational Publishers, Inc.

Cobrinik, L. (1974). Unusual reading ability in severely disturbed young children. *Journal of Autism and Childhood Schizophrenia*, 4, 163-175.

Committee on the Prevention of Reading Difficulties in Young Children. (1998). *Preventing reading difficulties in young children.* Washington, DC: National Academy Press.

Cunningham, J. W. (1993). Whole-to-part reading diagnosis. *Reading and Writing Quarterly: Overcoming Reading Difficulties*, 9 (1), 31-49.

Frith, U. & Snowling, M. (1983). Reading for meaning and reading for sound in autistic and dyslexic children. *British Journal of Developmental Psychology*, 1, 329-342.

Fry, E., Kress, J., & Fountoukidis, D. (2000). *The reading teacher's book of lists.* Paramus, New Jersey: Prentice Hall.

Mirenda, P. & Erickson, K. A. (2000). Augmentative communication and literacy. In A. Wetherby & B. Prizant (Eds.), *Autism spectrum disorders: A transactional developmental perspective* (pp. 333-367). Baltimore: Paul H. Brookes Publishing Co.

Picture Communication Symbols (PCS). (1981-2003). Solana Beach, CA: Mayer-Johnson.

Silberberg, N. E. & Silberberg, M. C. (1967). Hyperlexia: Specific word recognition skills in young children. *Exceptional Children*, 34, 41-42.

Texas Education Agency. (2000). *Texas reading initiative.* Austin, TX: TEA Publications.

Twachtman, D. D. (1995). Methods to enhance communication in verbal children. In Quill, K. A. (Ed.), *Teaching children with autism: Strategies to enhance communication and socialization* (pp. 133-162). New York: Delmar Publishers, Inc.